MARCH OF EMPEROR PENGUINS

BY BETH BENCE REINKE

The Child's World®
childsworld.com

Published by The Child's World®
1980 Lookout Drive • Mankato, MN 56003-1705
800-599-READ • www.childsworld.com

Photographs ©: Volt Collection/Shutterstock Images, cover, 1; Red Line Editorial, 5; Keith Szafranski/iStockphoto, 6, 14; iStockphoto, 9; Wolfgang Kaehler/Superstock/Glow Images, 10; Frans Lanting Mint Images/Newscom, 12; sheilapic76 CC2.0, 13; Solent News/Rex Features/AP Images, 17; Christopher Michel CC2.0, 18; Paula Jones/iStockphoto/Thinkstock, 20

ISBN 9781503816206

LCCN 2016945615

Printed in the United States of America
PA02319

TABLE OF CONTENTS

FAST FACTS

Name

- Emperor penguin (*Aptenodytes forsteri*)

Diet

- Emperor penguins eat **krill**, squid, and fish.
- To find fish and squid, emperor penguins can dive as deep as 1,800 feet (550 m).
- Emperor penguins can stay underwater for more than 20 minutes at a time.

Average Life Span

- Emperor penguins live for approximately 15 to 20 years.

Size

- Emperor penguins are the largest type of penguin.
- Emperor penguins can reach heights up to 45 inches (114 cm).

Weight

- Fully grown emperor penguins can weigh up to 88 pounds (40 kg).

Population

- There are approximately 595,000 emperor penguins in the world.
- Emperor penguins are a near-threatened species.

Where They're Found

- Emperor penguins live near the South Pole, on the coasts of Antarctica.

■ Emperor penguin habitats

Chapter 1

LAYING AN EGG

As winter begins at the South Pole, emperor penguins leave the sea. They leap out of the water onto an ice shelf. Then they stand up and start to walk away from the water. They plod across the uneven ice toward their **breeding grounds**.

It is -20 degrees Fahrenheit (-29°C). The penguins keep moving to keep warm. When the ice is smooth, the birds drop onto their bellies. They push with their feet and glide quickly over the white-blue ice.

After marching nonstop for almost a week, the penguins stop. They have traveled approximately 100 miles (160 km) inland. The ice is thick in this frozen place. The ice will not melt away, even in the summer.

◀ **As with all types of penguins, emperor penguins cannot fly.**

The penguins have found a place to breed. Each emperor chooses a mate.

Two months later, a mother penguin lays an egg. The light-green egg weighs only a pound (.45 kg). The mother uses her beak to push the egg off the icy ground and onto the top of her feet. She balances it there. Then she tucks it under a flap of her belly, called a **brood pouch**.

But now comes the tricky part. The mother must pass the egg to the father. The parents stand toe-to-toe. They have only one chance. If the egg cracks or freezes, the chick inside will die. Using their beaks and feet, they slowly push the egg onto the father's feet. He nestles it under his brood pouch to keep it warm.

The mother penguin joins the other female penguins that have given birth. They march back to the sea to find food. At the ice edge, the water is calm. The penguins plunge into the ocean headfirst. They gobble up fish and krill.

▲ Leopard seals can grow up to 12 feet
(3.7 m) long and are one of Antarctica's
top predators.

A hungry leopard seal prowls in the water nearby.
It opens its jaws wide, showing its sharp teeth. The
mother penguins dart away. The seal lunges forward,
but the penguins escape. They are safe for now.

Chapter 2

HATCHED!

For nine weeks, the father emperor cares for the egg. There is no sunlight, even during the day. But green, blue, and red **southern lights** dance in the sky overhead. The temperature drops to -50 degrees Fahrenheit (-46°C). The wind howls. But the egg is warm against the father's belly in the brood pouch.

The father stands upright day and night. It takes a lot of energy. He has had no food for more than three months. He is hungry, but there is nothing to eat in the frozen landscape. The father's body uses some of its **blubber** for energy. During blizzards, he bends down and picks up some snow. It melts in his mouth for a drink of water.

◄ To save energy, male emperor penguins may sleep for more than 20 hours in a day while standing with their eggs.

▲ Male penguins huddle together for warmth while protecting their eggs.

The father huddles together with other male penguins. They balance eggs on their feet, too. When the father is on the outside of the huddle, icy wind blows across his back. He waddles around to the side with less wind. As the males change places, they take turns in the middle, where it is warmer.

As winter fades, a bit of sunlight appears in the sky. Then one day, the father feels a jiggle on his feet.

A tiny hole appears in the egg. The chick inside the egg pecks at the shell. Soon it breaks out. The chick is only 5 inches (13 cm) tall. It is covered with fluffy gray down. The father pushes the chick under his brood pouch to keep it warm.

The baby is hungry. If the mother does not return soon with food, the chick might die. Will the mother return in time?

▲ Outside of the brood pouch, a chick can die from the cold within two minutes.

Chapter 3

WAITING GAME

A few days after the chick hatches, the mother arrives with a full belly. She bends her head down and opens her beak. The chick eats spit-up food from her mouth. Gently, the parents transfer the chick to its mother's feet. The chick snuggles into the mother's brood pouch. The family is together for a short time.

The sun gives more light each day, but it's still bitterly cold. The father begins his trek to the ocean. After not eating for four months, he is starving. He has lost almost half of his body weight. Sometimes, male emperor penguins are too weak and die before they reach the sea.

◄ An emperor penguin brings food up from its stomach to feed its chick.

Back at the breeding grounds, the little chick sits on the mother penguin's feet. The chick eats more spit-up fish from its mother's mouth. Soon, the chick grows big enough to leave the brood pouch. It learns to waddle on the ice. For a while, it stays close to its mother for warmth and safety. When it meets other chicks, they explore together.

A group of chicks wander onto rough ice. A **skua gull** swoops in. The big bird grabs one of the chicks in its claws and flies away. The mother of another chick waddles over to protect her baby. This time, her chick is safe.

In a few weeks, it is springtime. The chick is almost half as tall as its mother now. It has a bigger appetite than before.

The mother penguins must go fishing for more food. This time, the journey will not be as long. Warmer temperatures are melting the ice near the sea. Now, the open water is not as far away. The mothers march from the breeding grounds in a line.

▲ In bad weather, emperor penguin chicks form a crèche for warmth and protection.

Without its mother, the chick is helpless. But its father will return soon with more food. It huddles with other chicks, forming a **crèche** to stay warm.

Chapter 4

DIVING IN

The chicks hear trumpetlike calls. Male penguins waddle in a line from the sea. The chick hears a familiar voice. It is from the chick's father. The father spits up fish. The chick eats until its stomach is full.

The growing chick eats a lot. To bring the chick enough food, the mother and father take turns going fishing. If a seal or whale kills either parent, the chick will not have enough to eat. It will die, too.

Summer arrives. More ice melts into the sea. Now, the ocean is very near the breeding grounds. The penguin parents' job is done. One day, they leave the chick and go to the ocean to feed. The parents will not return.

◀ **An adult will feed only its own chick. The chick must recognize its parent's call in order to reunite and feed.**

▲ Down feathers keep emperor penguins warm. But chicks must grow waterproof feathers to survive in the water.

The big, fuzzy chick is on its own near the ice edge. But it cannot swim or catch fish yet. First, it must **molt** its feathers. The soft, gray ones slowly fall out. The chick waits, hungry, on the ice for many days. The chick would die in the cold, frosty ocean. It needs warm, waterproof feathers to protect it from the freezing water.

Little by little, new black and white feathers grow in. Finally, the chick has enough adult feathers to swim.

It dives into the ocean for the first time. The chicks will live at sea until they are five years old. Then they will be ready to mate.

The adult penguins molt their old feathers, too. It takes seven long weeks for new feathers to grow. Then the adults head out to sea. The emperors must fatten up for a long trip. Because when winter comes, the march to the breeding grounds will begin again.

THINK ABOUT IT

- Many emperor penguin chicks do not survive their first year. What risks do eggs and chicks face?
- Climate change may cause temperatures to rise in Antarctica. More ice would then melt. Penguins must sit on floating ice for seven weeks while they molt. If the floating ice melted too soon, what might happen?
- An emperor penguin's back is black like deep ocean water. Its belly is white like the sea ice. A leopard seal could swim above or below a penguin. How might the penguin's coloring protect it?

GLOSSARY

blubber (BLUB-ur): Blubber is fat under the skin of a marine animal. When they cannot eat for many days, emperor penguins use their blubber for energy.

breeding grounds (BREE-ding GROWNDZ): Breeding grounds are inland areas of ice where emperor penguins mate, hatch eggs, and raise chicks. It is a long, cold hike from the sea to the breeding grounds.

brood pouch (BREWD POWCH): A brood pouch is a thick flap of skin on a penguin's lower belly that covers an egg or chick. A chick stays warm in a brood pouch.

crèche (KRESH): A crèche is a group of penguin chicks standing close together for safety and warmth. Chicks spend time in the crèche when their parents are at sea.

krill (KRIL): Krill are tiny shrimp-like creatures that swim in the ocean. When emperor penguins dive into the ocean, they eat krill and fish.

molt (MOHLT): To molt is to lose a covering of fur, feathers, or hair and replace it with new growth. Emperor penguins molt their feathers once each year.

skua gull (SKOO-uh GUHL): A skua gull is a large sea bird that lives in Antarctica. Sometimes, skua gulls kill and eat penguin chicks.

southern lights (SUH-thurn LYTS): Southern lights are bands of colorful lights in the sky over the South Pole. Southern lights brighten the winter sky.

TO LEARN MORE

Books

London, Jonathan. *Little Penguin: The Emperor of Antarctica*. New York: Marshall Cavendish, 2011.

Miller, Sara Swan. *Emperor Penguins of the Antarctic*. New York: PowerKids, 2009.

Osborne, Mary Pope, and Natalie Pope Boyce. *Penguins and Antarctica*. New York: Random House, 2008.

Web Sites

Visit our Web site for links about emperor penguins: childsworld.com/links

Note to Parents, Teachers, and Librarians: We routinely verify our Web links to make sure they are safe and active sites. So encourage your readers to check them out!

SELECTED BIBLIOGRAPHY

"Emperor Penguin: Aptenodytes forsteri." *NationalGeographic*. National Geographic Partners, 2016. Web. 7 Jun. 2016.

"Emperor Penguins, Aptenodytes forsteri." *MarineBio.org*. MarineBio Conservation Society, n.d. Web. 7 Jun. 2016.

Kooyman, Gerald L., and Wayne Lynch. *Penguins: The Animal Answer Guide*. Baltimore, MD: Johns Hopkins UP, 2013. Print.

INDEX

ABOUT THE AUTHOR

Beth Bence Reinke is an animal lover with a bachelor's degree in biology education and a master's degree in nutrition. Her childhood dream of being a veterinarian was sidetracked by her allergy to cats. Instead, she is a registered dietitian, children's author, magazine writer, and a columnist for her favorite sport, NASCAR.